YOUR IDENTITY
in Christ

WHO YOU ARE AND WHOSE YOU ARE
31-Day Devotional

by ROBIN REVIS PYKE, PH.D.

WESTBOW
PRESS®
A DIVISION OF THOMAS NELSON
& ZONDERVAN

WestBow Press books may be ordered through booksellers or by contacting:

WestBow Press
A Division of Thomas Nelson & Zondervan
1663 Liberty Drive
Bloomington, IN 47403
www.westbowpress.com
844-714-3454

Interior Image Credit: Daria DiCieli

All Scripture quotations are taken from the World English Bible.

ISBN: 978-1-6642-8599-6 (sc)
ISBN: 978-1-6642-8600-9 (hc)
ISBN: 978-1-6642-8601-6 (e)

Library of Congress Control Number: 2022922526

Print information available on the last page.

WestBow Press rev. date: 03/02/2023

I Am
Joyful Peaceful
Redeemed
Gifted Strong Kind
Healed
Bold
Light
Righteous
Victorious
Tender
Forgiven Blessed Heard
Generous
Confident
Friend
Precious Anointed Seen
Servant
Respected
Beautiful Accepted
Enthusiastic
Faithful
Loved Worth
Chosen
Patient
Gentle
Energetic
Profitable
Alive Safe
Treasured
Kind Devout
Wise
Industrious
Blameless
Sanctified
Noble

Introduction

Do you find yourself questioning who you are meant to be or what your purpose is in life? Women around the world have been struggling with these thoughts for much too long, and you are far from alone in the search for your true identity. However, without the right foundation to begin from, you may never arrive at a fulfilling answer. As Christian women, we have to start with Christ. Once we fully appreciate who we are in God's greater plan, we can experience incredible spiritual growth and self-awareness unlike anything we've known before.

When you know your Creator and understand that God has given you life, you gain the fortitude to refuse to accept the labels the world attempts to impose upon you. You have the confidence and the bold faith to wear the crown God has destined for you, because you are chosen.

If you battle with your identity, you most likely base your value on or define who you are according to the world's standards. In today's world, you are surrounded by messages telling you who you should be or what you should believe in based on the thoughts and opinions of others. But this is not who God says you are, and the world's values are truly not up to God's standards or what He expects of us. God made you in His image, and He created your value and identity.

Your Identity in Christ: Who You Are and Whose You Are is a thirty-one-day devotional that will take you on a journey of self-discovery by utilizing the lasting truths found in the Bible. Who you are and whose you are will be unveiled as you work through this powerful message of hope while uncovering the truths of what the Word of God says about your value and showing the true picture of who you are and whose you are.

Understanding your identity in Christ is a breath of fresh air for an overwhelmed soul and life-changing. When you truly grasp the gift of God's amazing grace, it brings hope to even the deepest doubter, and it is there where the weary soul finds a reprieve from the struggles that threaten to consume your thoughts. It is there where the shameful woman finds redemption from her past and dares to start again. And it is there where fear is banished, and you discover how God's Word defines you.

Your identity is found in Christ, not your feelings, achievements, or the material things of this world. God's truth reminds you of your identity and where your worth comes from. You are a daughter of the King. Our Heavenly Father wholly and completely loves you.

Are you ready to embrace your identity and let go of the false identities you hold on to? For the next thirty-one days, I pray you will embrace God's Word and His promises. Accept His Truth and allow His Words to fill your soul. I encourage you to begin each day reading these biblical truths about who you are and whose you are and allow God's Word to transform you. He is the way, the truth, and the life (John 14:6).

You Are His Workmanship

For we are his workmanship, created in Christ Jesus for good
works, which God prepared before that we would walk in them.

—EPHESIANS 2:10

When you meet someone new, how do you identify yourself? What are some of the first things you want people to know about you? For example, do you say, "Hi, my name is Robin, and I'm a writer"? Or do you lead with, "Hi, I'm Debby, and I'm married with three children"? Maybe you don't say it quite that quickly. But, often, how we identify ourselves in the first moments of meeting someone tells others what we believe is important about ourselves. Likewise, the questions we ask others when we first meet them tell them what we will value about them, such as "What do you do?," "Where do you work?," or "Where did you go to school?" As humans, we tend to value people according to their relationships, titles, or accomplishments. But your identity is so much more than that.

In God's economy, your identity is not based on your relationships. You are not valuable to God because you are someone's wife, mother, sister, daughter, or friend. Yes, relationships are essential, as God created us to be both in relationship with Him and with one another, but that's not where our value lies. Finding our identities in being the best wife, best mom, or best friend is not solid ground to stand on because human relationships are fragile. When we build our identities on our relationships, the possible loss of connection could be something we may not recover from.

The same is true of basing our identities on our abilities or contributions to the world. When we uphold these things as the marker for who we are, what happens when someone more intelligent, more prosperous, or more beautiful comes along? We become confused, lost, or even competitive. We must not base our identities on how we measure up to others. Comparison is unhealthy for us since the target is constantly moving, which means we will never be content.

So if we are not what we do, what we contribute, or whom we know, who are we? God's Word clearly defines who we are and whose we are, and for the next thirty days, we are going to discover our identities in Christ. Be prepared to experience freedom and power you never knew existed.

Reflection

1. Reflecting on Ephesians 2:10, what does it mean to you to know that you are God's workmanship, created for His purpose?

2. What ways have you identified yourself in the past, and how do you currently identify yourself? Now that you know you are God's workmanship, will this understanding change how you identify yourself moving forward?

Jesus, Your Savior

Not by works of righteousness which we did ourselves, but according to his mercy, he saved us through the washing of regeneration and renewing by the Holy Spirit, whom he poured out on us richly, through Jesus Christ our Savior.

—Titus 3:5–6

To fully understand who we are, we must first understand who Jesus is. Of course, we all "know" who Jesus is, to some degree. He's the Son of God, the second person in the Trinity who came to earth, fully man and fully God, to live a sinless life. He died on the cross for our sins, and on the third day, He rose again, conquering death and the grave on our behalf. Jesus sits at the right hand of the Father, awaiting God's command to come and get His bride, the church. But to ultimately know who we are in Him, we need to know and understand His character.

Jesus is our Savior. Simply put, a savior is someone who saves another person from something. We often throw around the phrases, "You saved me!" or "You saved my life!" or "That's a lifesaver," but the truth is Jesus *did* save us. What did He save us from? Our sin. Sin is our act of disobedience to God. Sometimes these are things we do that He has said not to do, but sometimes these are things we don't do that He has commanded us to do. Sin is a factor of being human, and we are all sinners. Romans 3:23 says, "For all have sinned, and fall short of the glory of God."

As hard as it is to admit, there are days when I seem to easily fall into disobedience. Despite my desire to walk in obedience, it is usually the small things that lead me to disobey. Whether the temptation is too great and I just can't help myself, or I allow the world's noise to influence my decisions, I know better and genuinely want to do better. There's a fundamental lesson here—there are always consequences when we submit to our desires.

Why do we need to be saved from our sin? Romans 6:23 tells us, "For the wages of sin is death, but the free gift of God is eternal life in Christ Jesus our Lord." The cost for our sin is death, which eternally separates us from God. The good news is that Jesus died in our place so we wouldn't have to! He *saved* us from eternal death and brought us *into* eternal life! Because He died in our place, we have direct, everlasting access to a holy God and will live with Him in heaven after our time on earth ends. As a result, we should live our lives in a perpetual state of humble gratitude for what He did for us. Jesus is our Savior!

Reflection

1. Reflecting on today's verse, are there any areas in your life where you may be walking in disobedience to God? If so, ask God to release you from any obstacles or waywardness hindering your spiritual growth.

2. What are some ways to express your gratitude to Jesus, your Savior, today? Consider keeping a gratitude journal to express your thanks and praise God for all that He has done and continues to do for you.

Jesus, Your Redeemer

Who gave himself for us, that he might redeem us from all iniquity, and purify for himself a people for his own possession, zealous for good works.

—TITUS 2:14

Before we dive into who we are, let's look at who Jesus is since our identities exist in relation to Him. Yesterday, we learned that He is our Savior and that He has saved us *from* our sin, bringing us *into* eternal life. Today, let's take a look at Jesus, our Redeemer.

What is a redeemer? To redeem means to "buy back," so a redeemer is a person who buys back, repurchases, or clears a debt. In the book of Ruth, we see an example of what this looks like from an earthly perspective. Ruth was a woman who lived in a time when the judges ruled Israel. She was not an Israelite, but she married one. Her mother-in-law was Naomi, and when both Ruth's and Naomi's husbands died, it left them entirely destitute. They owned nothing and had no source of income, nowhere to live, and no food to eat.

Boaz, a man born out of the family line of Naomi's late husband, was their kinsman. Seeing Ruth and Naomi struggling, he allowed them to glean food from his field, which afforded them the luxury of eating until they were satisfied. Later, Boaz married Ruth and bought back the fields that Naomi's husband had once owned and gifted them back to her. So Boaz became their earthly kinsman-redeemer, their restorer, provider, and sustainer.

Jesus is our Redeemer. Because He paid the price of death for our sin, He has purchased us back from the sin that enslaved us. Titus 2:14 says, "Who gave himself for us, that he might redeem us from all iniquity, and purify for himself a people for his own possession, zealous for good works." Not only did Jesus redeem us to be free from our sin, but He also purchased us in order to transform us into people who are zealous to do good. In Revelation 5:9, "they sang a new song, saying, 'You are worthy to take the book and to open its seals: for you were killed, and bought us for God with your blood out of every tribe, language, people, and nation.'" Our Redeemer bought us to save us from our sin, to enable us to do good deeds, and to allow us to spend eternity with God in heaven. Like Job, we can say, "I know my Redeemer lives!" (Job 19:25). Jesus's redemption pardons us and gives us hope for eternity.

Reflection

1. Being redeemed means that we are free from the sin that held us captive. Is there sin in your life that is still enslaving you even though Jesus has fully redeemed you from it? If so, ask Him to reveal that sin to you and remove it from your life today. Freedom from sin is yours for the asking!

2. Being redeemed also means that we were purchased to become people who are passionate about doing good. Do you have a passion for doing good? If not, ask your Redeemer to help you fully comprehend your redemption and give you a desire to do good to everyone.

Jesus, Your Light

Again, therefore, Jesus spoke to them, saying, "I am the light of the world. He who follows me will not walk in the darkness, but will have the light of life."

—John 8:12

Jesus is our Savior and our Redeemer. Today, we'll talk about Jesus, our Light. John 8:12 says, "Again, therefore, Jesus spoke to them, saying, 'I am the light of the world. He who follows me will not walk in the darkness, but will have the light of life.'"

On the first day of creation, God said, "Let there be light," and it appeared. As soon as these words came out of the mouth of God, illumination broke through the surrounding shadows at approximately 186,000 miles per second. This was the first separation between light and darkness, the separation of holiness and sin. God ordered the light to shine through the night. The very voice of God was powerful enough to make this happen, and Jesus was right there as it did. John 1:2 tells us that Jesus "was in the beginning with God." In Revelation, we learn that there is no need for light in heaven because God is the light of heaven. Similarly, Jesus describes Himself as the Light of the world. The light we will experience in heaven is of God, but any light we encounter here on earth is of Jesus.

I find it comforting to know that Jesus promises that anyone who chooses to walk with Him will not walk in the darkness but will have the Light—His Light—that leads to life. These words assure me that although there is darkness (sin) in the world, to follow Him is to walk in the light and live life in the fullness of Christ. I believe that when we do so, it will be reflected through us so that others may follow Him.

Psalm 119:105 tells us that God's Word is a lamp to our feet and a light to our path. God's Word lights the way for our journey. We choose which path we take; however, if we commit our ways to the Lord and choose righteousness, we will not stumble. Instead, our pathways will be illuminated so we can walk confidently, knowing that He directs our steps. Our journeys can be testimonies to others who desire to walk in Jesus's light!

Walking in the light means we live our lives in a way that honors God. It means fleeing from sin and pursuing holiness. It is about being a new creation and leaving the person we were before behind in favor of following Christ. And we do this because we have the hope of salvation, the hope of the cross, and the hope that Jesus will come again to make all things new.

Reflection

1. Has there been a time in your life when you experienced walking from darkness into the light?

2. Light is critical for life. So today, thank Jesus for providing you with life-giving light, both physically and spiritually.

Jesus, Your Shepherd

I am the good shepherd. I know my own, and I'm known by my own; even as the Father knows me, and I know the Father. I lay down my life for the sheep.

—JOHN 10:14–15

John 10:14 is one of seven "I Am" statements in the Bible. In this verse, Jesus declares, "I am the good shepherd." We interpret this as Him explaining that He takes care of His flock, providing for His followers physically, mentally, and spiritually.

Shepherding was a common practice in Jesus's day. Shepherds served in the fields where they watched over their sheep, safeguarding the herd by providing food and water, protecting it from predators, and leading it to safety. The flock of sheep placed their utmost trust in their shepherd. They trust the shepherd to take care of their needs daily, and they follow their leader, knowing they can rely on him.

As our Shepherd, Jesus makes sure that we, His flock, have plenty of spiritual food and water and that we can find it when we seek it. He watches over us without rest and knows each of us so well that He calls us by name. Most importantly, in John 10:14–15, Jesus compares His relationship with us as one in alignment with His relationship with His Father: " … even as the Father knows me, and I know the Father." These words emphasize just how much Jesus loves and cares for us. His Word assures us that if we follow Him, He will lay down His life for us.

Are you comforted knowing that Jesus, the Good Shepherd, will leave the entire flock to locate one who has strayed? Do you find security in the fact that Jesus will lay down His life for you? I know that when I feel abandoned or lost in life, I can be assured that when I cry out to Jesus, the ever-faithful Shepherd will answer my call because I am His, and He is mine. I can trust that Jesus will bring me faithfully back to the flock.

To know His voice and recognize that Jesus, our Shepherd, will safeguard us on our journey is a salve to my soul. Our Shepherd would willingly lay down His life to save us because He is good. He did just that so we could find rest in His presence.

Reflection

1. The shepherd oversees the flock to keep it from harm. In return, the sheep within the herd know the shepherd's voice and comply with his requests for safety and protection. Jesus, the Good Shepherd, watches over His flock as well. As a believer, do you follow Jesus and walk in obedience to His direction?

2. When you are lost or stray too far off the narrow path, who is the first person you call out to or run to for protection or safety?

Jesus, Your Everything

For of him, and through him, and to him are all things. To him be the glory forever! Amen.

—ROMANS 11:36

*J*esus is our everything. The Bible says:

1. Jesus is our everything because everything, including you, originates with Him (Romans 11:36). Our identity is rooted in Christ because we began in Him, and we were also created in the Father's image because He and the Father are one (John 10:30). We are not our own; we are His.

2. Jesus is our everything because He provides everything we need. "My God will supply every need of yours according to his riches in glory in Christ Jesus" (Philippians 4:19). What we own or can earn was not provided by us; they are gifts from God. He provided the income necessary to make way for all blessings. Your things are not your own; they are His.

3. Jesus is our everything because He gives us power. Philippians 4:13 says, "I can do all things through Christ, who strengthens me." What we perceive to be our contributions are, in actuality, the accomplishments we were able to achieve

because of the power of Christ in us. Apart from Jesus, we can do nothing (John 15:5). Our strength is not our own; it is His.

4. Jesus is our everything because He gives us victory. "No, in all these things, we are more than conquerors through him who loved us" (Romans 8:37). Not only has He already conquered sin and death on our behalf as our Savior, but the book of Romans tells us that we also conquer all things through Him. Our victories are not ours; they are His.

When Jesus is our everything, we understand and accept that all we do and have is through Him. Jesus provides for us. He gives us the strength to do His will. We do not make things happen as a result of our strength but because of His. We base our identities on what He has done and will continue to do in us and through us. We are not our own; we are His.

Reflection

1. Are you in a partial relationship with Jesus? Is Jesus your hope in all areas of your life or only some? Is He your everything? Today, ask Him to reveal places where you have held Him at arm's length, and then invite Him into those spaces. Lean into His provision, His strength, and His victory.

2. Have you believed the lies of the enemy who tells you that you are unloved, unwanted, or a disappointment? Today, surrender those lies for God's Truth. Anchor your identity in who God says you are—a beautiful woman created by Him in His image to live life in the victory of Christ.

Jesus, Your Source for Forgiveness

Therefore if anyone is in Christ, he is a new creation. The old things have passed away. Behold, all things have become new.

—2 Corinthians 5:17

Now that we know who Jesus is, let's reflect on our relationship with Him, our connection to Him, and how we relate to Him. At the most basic level, we recognize that we are sinners in need of saving, and Jesus is the One who saves. Romans 5:8 says, "But God commends his own love toward us, in that while we were yet sinners, Christ died for us." Jesus's death provides forgiveness for our sins, a complete erasure of anything we've ever done. The Bible says that God separates us from our sins as far as the east is from the west (Psalm 103:12) and remembers them no more. Jesus's death makes it possible for our sins to disappear so that we experience no condemnation from God (Romans 8:1–2).

Not only are our sins forgiven, but we are also forgiven and made new. "Therefore if anyone is in Christ, he is a new creation. The old things have passed away. Behold, all things have become new" (2 Corinthians 5:17). Our old, sinful selves die and make way for our new lives in Christ. Water baptism is a beautiful picture of this. As we go under the water, it symbolizes death to our old lives, just as being raised from the water displays that we are made new again. When we recognize who we are as sinners and that Jesus not only saved us so that we could spend eternity with Him but also to make us completely new, we can be strengthened and encouraged.

As you reflect on your life, do not allow your past to define you. Most of us have struggled at times over our past choices, wondering where we would be today if we had not strayed from the path set before us. But, my sweet friend, let me remind you of the good news that when you accept Jesus Christ as your Savior, you are entirely forgiven for your transgressions! Therefore, there is no reason to dwell on your past sins. Instead, I encourage you to be confident in God's love for you because, in Christ, your sins have been wiped away, and you have been made new!

Reflection

1. As you reflect on 2 Corinthians 5:17, are there any areas of the past that you continue to dwell on or are allowing to define who you are today?

2. How has your perception changed regarding how you relate to Jesus since becoming a new creation and learning He is the source of your forgiveness and transformation?

Jesus, Your Source for Purpose

If anyone, therefore, purges himself from these, he will be a vessel for honor, sanctified, and suitable for the master's use, prepared for every good work.

—2 TIMOTHY 2:21

Being "in Christ" reflects how we view Jesus and how we relate to Him through our sense of self and identity. Once our sins have been removed, Jesus gives us new purpose, and we become transformed creatures who are free to do good works.

We were designed to thrive in our purpose. Many women spend a lot of time, money, and effort seeking purpose in their lives. However, those who are in Christ don't have to look very hard, because He provides it freely through His redemption and His light in our lives.

God tells us we were put on earth for a specific purpose: to proclaim His praises and to spread His message, the Good News. God called us out of the darkness and brought us into His kingdom of glorious light.

We often run about seeking our calling and trying to make things happen in our own strength. Unfortunately, some people spend their entire lives searching for true purpose, waiting on God to call them to something when He has already laid the path before them.

God has called each of us to a specific task and has given us unique talents and gifts according to His will. However, all Christ-followers have some assignments in common. (1) We are to tell people about Jesus and make disciples (Matthew 28:19–20). (2) We are to bear the fruit of the Spirit that lives in us (Galatians 5:22–23). (3) We are to walk in unity with each other (Ephesians 4:13). (4) We are to mature in our faith through prayer, the study of His Word, and Christian community (1 Corinthians 3:1–2). (5) We are to be set apart and prepared to do good works (2 Timothy 2:21).

If you are discouraged or unsure of your purpose, I encourage you to surrender and seek the work God has put in front of you. Let go of the stress of trying to figure out your calling. Stop striving to make things happen in your strength. My friend, if you're forcing yourself to be someone or something you are not comfortable with, you may be trying to accomplish something that is not your purpose. Surrendering to God in a simple act of obedience is the first step in fulfilling your unique calling. Go to your Father.

Reflection

1. What are some things in your life that you once considered to be your purpose that may not have been? Were you striving to make it happen in your own strength?

2. Take a moment and reflect on the impact you are making. You were uniquely created to contribute to the world. Ask God if there is anything in your life that is hindering you from completing the good work He has planned for you.

Jesus, Your Source for Peace

Peace I leave with you. My peace I give to you; not as the world gives, I give to you. Don't let your heart be troubled, neither let it be fearful.

—JOHN 14:27

Our world is full of things that make us afraid. World disasters, pandemics, looming financial crises, and more can create an anxious and afraid spirit within us. If that's not enough, there are media and entertainment sources dedicated to instilling more fear into the population. But know this: the Prince of Peace did not redeem us so that we would live our lives in fear.

Jesus Himself told His disciples that this world would not be a place of peace but that, in Him, they would have peace. They could hold on to this promise because He has overcome the world. Christ alone gives us perfect peace—not the world, our achievements, or material things. The peace of Christ will calm our fears and comfort us in times of adversity.

Because Jesus is the Prince of Peace (Isaiah 9:6), He is the spring from which any peace we experience begins. In John 14:27, Jesus said, "Peace I leave with you. My peace I give to you; not as the world gives, I give to you. Don't let your heart be troubled, neither let it be fearful." The world tries in many ways to offer us peace and quiet. From spa days to vacations to medications, the world has many techniques that claim to bring us shalom. But Jesus said that all of these things combined could not compare to the peace He can give us when we ask.

You might say, "Jesus is not here on earth with us anymore. How can He provide me peace when He is in a perfect heaven while I am on chaotic earth?" The answer is this: He sent His Holy Spirit to provide for us in His place until He returns. One of the many roles of the Holy Spirit is to be our Comforter (John 14:16), to provide us the peace that passes all understanding—even in the middle of chaos. When on earth, Jesus calmed the storms and the demon-possessed, the families of the ill, and even His own followers as He went to the cross.

Today, through His Spirit, we have access to that same source of solace so that when we are in the midst of the storms, we may rest in the comfort of God. Shalom.

Reflection

1. Are there any areas in your life where you sense a lack of peace? Take time to pray through those areas and surrender the unrest to God. As you surrender, seek His perfect peace and spend time praying this Scripture, "Search me, God, and know my heart. Try me, and know my thoughts. See if there is any wicked way in me, and lead me in the everlasting way (Psalm 139:23-24).

2. Pondering on the peace God gives, reflect on a time where you experienced God's peace. How does God's peace differ from the temporary peace of the world?

In the Beginning

In the beginning was the Word, and the Word was with God, and the Word was God.

—John 1:1

In this verse, John is identifying Jesus Christ as the Word of God. The Bible clearly defines who we are, which is why it is essential to our spiritual growth that we spend time daily reading the Word. God's Word solidifies our identity in Christ. As we grow in our faith, we transition from relying on the milk of spiritual infancy to the more substantial sustenance of spiritual maturity. Studying the Word of God is key to understanding who He is, what He stands for, how He defines us, and what He expects from us.

The Bible is the inspired Word of God, written by many authors over the course of many, many years. Scholars attribute the writings of these men to the Holy Spirit as they were filled with God's Spirit when the books were authored.

The Bible contains sixty-six books—thirty-nine books in the Old Testament and twenty-seven books in the New Testament. The Old Testament begins with the Pentateuch, the first five books, which tell the story of creation and the beginning of God's nation of Israel. The remainder of the books in the Old Testament describe the ongoing story of Israel, either through history, prophecy, or song. The New Testament begins with the Gospels: Matthew, Mark,

Luke, and John. Each of these writers tells the story of Jesus's life on earth from a slightly different perspective. Next is Acts, which tells the story of the early church. Followed by that is a series of letters from various authors to the Church. They give us insight into how God wants Christ-followers to live. Finally, Revelation prophesies the end of days.

John 1:14 tell us, "The Word became flesh, and lived among us. We saw his glory, such glory as of the one and only Son of the Father, full of grace and truth." Jesus *is* the Word of God. The Bible tells the story of Jesus from beginning to end. He was with God from beginning to end, and He will return to make everything new again. If we are to understand who we are in Him, we must take time to get to know His story—the greatest story ever to be told.

Reflection

1. Studying God's Word is essential to our spiritual growth. What steps can you take today to ensure daily reading and studying of God's Word?

2. As you study God's Word, pray God will give you the wisdom and knowledge to apply His Word to your life, deepening your spiritual growth.

The Word of God

For the word of God is living and active, and sharper than any two-edged sword, piercing even to the dividing of soul and spirit, of both joints and marrow, and is able to discern the thoughts and intentions of the heart.

—Hebrews 4:12

The study of God's Word is commanded of us because it lights our path forward and transforms us from the inside out. Paul said to Timothy, "Give diligence to present yourself approved by God, a workman who doesn't need to be ashamed, properly handling the Word of Truth" (2 Timothy 2:15). Being a disciple requires discipline, and disciplined study of scripture allows us to share God's Word—the truth—with others and guards against false teaching.

How do we start? When studying the Word of God, it is essential to begin each session in prayer. I begin by inviting the Holy Spirit into my space. I pray for God's Word to speak to me, and I ask God to reveal any areas of my life where I need to apply His truth. Most importantly, as I create a sacred space for God to meet with me, I ask the Holy Spirit to free me from any distractions or worldly noise.

As you begin spending time in God's Word, I recommend starting with the Gospels. The Gospels are the first four books of the New Testament: Matthew, Mark, Luke, and John. Each book tells the story of Jesus's life from a different perspective. As disciples of Jesus

Christ, it is significant to our journey to know our Savior and Master. Why? Because we must filter everything that others say about us and what we say about ourselves through the lens of scripture. If we do not know the Word of God, how can we interpret the messages of the world? How will we know if what we are hearing is from God? Knowing God's Word allows us to discern His voice and determine if what we are hearing aligns with His Word.

Therefore, it is significant to our spiritual growth that we know and lean on God's Word and who God says we are. And, my dear friends, we can only do this through studying the Bible. Spending time in God's Word is essential to our belief that we can become who we were created to be. The Bible is the only infallible source of wisdom and truth in this broken world, and we must take time every day to get into scripture and remind ourselves who we truly are.

Reflection

1. Reflecting on today's scripture, what does it mean to you to know that the Word of God is alive and powerful?

2. Have there been any times in your life when you may have fallen for or been exposed to false teachings? If so, ask God to free you of those messages and ask God to increase your knowledge so that you may be on guard against false doctrine.

What the Lord Requires of You

He has shown you, O man, what is good. What does Yahweh require of you, but to act justly, to love mercy, and to walk humbly with your God?

—MICAH 6:8

It's often hard to figure out what God wants from us. I've said many times that I wish He would just send me an email with His requests. I would do whatever He asked if He would just spell it out for me in black and white. But God doesn't communicate that way. Instead, He speaks to us through His Word and His Spirit. So, while I can't decipher His specific messages for you as He speaks to you through His Spirit, I can guide you through what His Word says He requires of us.

1. He wants us to follow Him. Much like He commanded the original twelve disciples in Matthew 4:19, "He said to them, 'Come after me, and I will make you fishers for men.'" Jesus calls us today to cast our nets for people.
2. He wants us to focus on Him. Following Jesus means keeping our eyes fixed on Him. When Jesus was walking on water, He commanded Peter to come to him. Peter stepped out of the boat to walk to Jesus. In one brief moment, he allowed fear to overcome him and began to sink (Matthew 14:28).

You see, as long as Peter kept his eyes focused on His Master, he stayed upright. But as soon as he took his eyes off Jesus, he lost his footing and nearly drowned. The same is true of us. When we keep our eyes on Jesus (Hebrews 12:2), the Author and Perfector of our faith, we can achieve things that may seem impossible. When we look away, though—even for a moment—we are in danger of being consumed by a sea of distractions in this world.

3. He wants you to fulfill your unique purpose. God has created only one of you, and no one can take your place. You are unique and set apart for His purpose. When our purpose goes unfulfilled, we miss out on the blessing that is living a life of purpose.

4. He wants us to trust Him (Proverbs 3:5–6). He is always in control. When we seem to be surrounded by chaos and unable to see a way forward, we should acknowledge Him. He will make our paths straight. He is who He says He is and will do what He says He will do, always.

What does God require of you? He commands you to do what is right, love one another, and walk humbly with Him.

Reflection

1. Are you leading a God-centered life? Are you humbly following Him? If not, what are the things that distract you?

2. Micah 6:8 says God requires us to act justly, love mercifully, and walk humbly with Him. With which of those do you most struggle? Confess your challenges to God (He already knows), and ask Him to help you overcome obstacles so you can live in the victory of Christ today.

What Do You Stand For?

Yes, and for this very cause adding on your part all diligence, in your faith supply moral excellence; and in moral excellence, knowledge; and in knowledge, self-control; and in self-control perseverance; and in perseverance godliness; and in godliness brotherly affection; and in brotherly affection, love.

—2 PETER 1:5–7

esus did not save us only to have us fall prey to the ever-changing tides of false teachings and popular opinion. We have the responsibility to live out the expectations of God and reflect His truth in our words and behavior. As disciples of Jesus Christ, *we* are to stand for what *He* stands for, and because we know and love Him, we serve Him.

Second Peter 1:5–7 tells us what we should stand for when it says, "Yes, and for this very cause adding on your part all diligence, in your faith supply moral excellence; and in moral excellence, knowledge; and in knowledge, self-control; and in self-control perseverance; and in perseverance godliness; and in godliness brotherly affection; and in brotherly affection, love." We should reflect the character traits listed in this passage in our thoughts and daily actions. God calls us to these standards as followers of Christ. God did the work of redeeming us—something we could not do for ourselves. Therefore, we should willingly do the work He has called us to do. This includes the common purposes we share, our individually gifted purposes, and the careful and persistent pursuit of faith, moral excellence (virtue), knowledge, self-control (temperance), perseverance (patience), godliness, kindness, and love (charity).

God expects us to pursue these things in our lives diligently in response to the immeasurable gift He has given us. Therefore, our responsibility is to seek a righteous life by cultivating these attributes in sisterly love toward one another to confirm our calling and to reflect God's qualities back at those we are called to serve.

Reflection

1. As you consider the list from 2 Peter 1:5–7, which of these qualities do you most reflect in your daily walk? Are any of the attributes listed in the scripture a struggle for you? If so, ask God to help you identify ways you can increase the use of these attributes in your life.

2. Is there anything you are pursuing in your life that is in opposition to these characteristics? What steps can you take today to release yourself from this bondage?

You Are Faithful

Now faith is assurance of things hoped for, proof of things not seen.

—HEBREWS 11:1

O ur faith in God is the bedrock of our foundation. Over and over in the book of Revelation, Jesus is called "Faithful and True" (Revelation 3:14, 19:11, 21:5). In Revelation 17:14, the Bible says, "And those who are with Him [that's us!] are the called and chosen and faithful." It's God's job to do the calling and the choosing, but it's our job to remain faithful. Jesus stands for faithfulness, and because we are His disciples, we do too.

To know what it means to be faithful or full of faith, we must first understand what faith is. "Now faith is the assurance of things hoped for, proof of things not seen" (Hebrews 11:1). Simply put, faith is being sure of the eternal hope we have put in Jesus, even though we have never seen Him. The eleventh chapter of Hebrews, a chapter often called the "Faith Hall of Fame," highlights biblical heroes—men and women—who were filled with faith. Even though they could not see God, they moved in obedience to His commands because they believed that He would keep His promises.

These heroes include men like Noah and Abraham and women like Sarah and Rahab. They did what God called them to do in great faith, at times risking their own lives. In many cases, they did not even live long enough to see God make good on His promises. However, because they understood that God's timeline is not limited to man's lifetime, they moved forward knowing that future generations would be blessed and that they themselves would secure eternal rest and reward.

Like these faithful and true followers of Christ, we can confidently place our faith in God. Whatever He has asked you to do, say yes, and be obedient to the call. He will never leave you. "If we are faithless, He remains faithful; for He can't deny Himself" (2 Timothy 2:13). Therefore, we are encouraged to persevere through faith. We will find victory through our confidence in Christ when we believe and apply His Word to our lives because it only takes faith the size of a mustard seed for God to show up!

Reflection

1. Reflecting on Hebrews 11:1, what or who are you placing your faith in? Based on your response, what is your next step to place your faith and hope in Jesus Christ?

2. Are there any areas of your life in which your faith has wavered? If so, ask God to strengthen the foundation of your faith.

You Are Knowledge

For if these things are yours and abound, they make you to not be idle or unfruitful in the knowledge of our Lord Jesus Christ.
—2 PETER 1:8

One of the ways we grow in our relationship with Jesus and understand our identity in Him is by gaining knowledge. All humans grow in knowledge as we age and mature. Over time, we learn new skills and increase our wisdom with each phase of life. *The Believer's Bible Commentary* states, "There is either advance or decline in the pathway of discipleship - no standing still."

In 2 Peter 1:5–7, Peter lists the characteristics Christians should diligently pursue. "In your faith supply moral excellence; and in moral excellence, knowledge; and in knowledge, self-control; and in self-control perseverance; and in perseverance godliness; and in godliness brotherly affection; and in brotherly affection, love."

First and foremost, disciples of Jesus should gain knowledge of who He is. In 2 Peter 1:8, Peter says, "For if these things are yours and abound, they make you to not be idle or unfruitful in the knowledge of our Lord Jesus Christ." To be useful and fruitful in the kingdom of God, we must acquire these traits in order to understand Jesus better. While it's popular these days to have a spiritual experience led by emotions, if we only engage in heart-based encounters with Him, it may cause us to love a Jesus we don't know very well. Consequently, when we don't know who Jesus is, we can't fully comprehend who we are in Him.

When we gain clarity on who God is and continue to increase our knowledge of God's Word, the foundation of our identity becomes stronger, which allows us to gain a clearer picture of who we are, what we're worth, and where we're going.

As daughters of the King, we are wholly and completely loved by our heavenly Father. These words are powerful! We spend a lot of time, effort, and money trying to fill ourselves up with material possessions, professional accomplishments, and relationships. But the truth of Christ is more than enough to fill us to overflowing. The knowledge of Jesus Christ reinforces our faith and increases our spiritual growth. You are knowledge!

Reflection

1. Do you know who Jesus is? If someone were to ask you, "Who is Jesus?", what would you say?

2. In what ways do you diligently pursue knowledge? Has your learning increased your faith walk?

You Are Filled with the Fruit of the Spirit

But the fruit of the Spirit is love, joy, peace, patience, kindness, goodness, faith, gentleness, and self-control. Against such things there is no law. Those who belong to Christ have crucified the flesh with its passions and lusts.

—GALATIANS 5:22-24

What does it mean when we say that a character quality is a fruit of the Spirit? It simply means that those are the virtues we display when the Spirit of God lives in us. God has promised us that when we are in a relationship with Christ, His Spirit lives in us. One way others recognize Jesus within us and the transformation in our lives is how the fruit of the Spirit shows itself in our words and actions.

As I meet with remarkable women who have a deep desire to step into their calling, we discuss the qualities we need to reflect on as we serve. These very virtues are found in Galatians 5:22–23: love, joy, peace, forbearance, kindness, goodness, faithfulness, gentleness, and self-control.

Jesus's life is the exemplary model of producing the fruit of the Spirit. And it is Jesus Christ who states in Matthew 7:20, "Therefore by their fruits, you will know them."

When people look at you, what fruits will they see from your actions and words? Will they see kindness, faithfulness, and love? As followers of Christ, we must step into all that God has for us, and that includes exhibiting these characteristics in our lives as we reflect on Him. To do this, we must display character qualities pleasing to God, including willingness to exercise self-control, gentleness, and patience as we pursue our purpose. We must honor God with our choices and behaviors.

Do you want to say yes to living a life filled with the virtuous fruit of the Holy Spirit? If so, you will need to lay down anything that produces bitter fruit because you cannot walk fully with God while living a me-centered life.

Reflection

1. What type of fruit are you bearing in your life?

2. Are there any strongholds in your life that you need to surrender so that you may live a life filled with the fruit of the Spirit?

The Way, the Truth, and the Life

Jesus said to him, "I am the way, the truth, and the life. No one comes to the Father, except through me."

—JOHN 14:6

If it were charted on a timeline, a Christian's walk would have three main parts: justification, salvation, and sanctification.

In justification we are saved from the penalty of our sins (Romans 5:1); Salvation is the point at which we begin our relationship with Jesus (Philippians 2:12). This is when we realize we are sinners, repent, and declare Him to be our Lord. This special moment is considered to be our spiritual birthday. Sanctification is the process that lasts from the time of salvation until our time on earth ends. These are our growing-up-in-Jesus years.

Sanctification is the pursuit of godliness, always keeping the end in mind. We begin our journeys as spiritual infants and walk toward eternity, where we will be glorified, whole, and godly versions of ourselves. Godliness consists of two parts: knowing God (through the study of His Word and careful observation of His work in our lives) and living a holy, set-apart life (sanctification).

The journey of sanctification is our path to increasing godliness. The goal of a Christian is to be more like Jesus at the end of her life than she was at the moment of salvation by making incremental improvements day after day.

Not to simplify the significance of salvation, but it's similar to gardening. You prepare the field, plant the seeds, and nurture the soil, depending on the type of seeds and climate. As you maintain the planted seeds, it may be difficult to tell if the seeds will produce the harvest you planned, but after a time, you will begin to see the yield of your crops. Your harvest may not be visible in the day-to-day, but over time, as you continue to grow spiritually, the fruits of your labor will be evident to both God and those around you. The fruit that glorifies God is everlasting. "He is the way, the truth, and the life" (John 14:6).

Reflection

1. Salvation is available to any person who is ready to serve and trust God. Are you serving God today? If you believe God's Word and His Truth are the way to salvation and you are ready to make the decision to follow Him, I encourage you to pray this simple prayer and ask God to enter your heart.

   Dear Lord,

   I admit that I am a sinner. I have done many things that are not pleasing to you. I have lived my life for myself only. I am sorry, and I repent. I ask you to forgive me.

   I believe that you died on the cross for me, to save me. Therefore, from this day forward, help me to live every day for you and in a way that is obedient to you.

   I love you, Lord, and I thank you that I will spend all eternity with you.

   Amen

*If you sincerely prayed that prayer, know that the Spirit of God now lives inside you, as He has promised in His Word. Seek out a local, Bible-believing church for baptism and the next steps in your discipleship.

Who Does God Say You Are?

God created man in his own image. In God's image he created him; male and female he created them

—Genesis 1:27

So far, we've learned that we are *not* our accomplishments, our relationships, or what we can acquire. We've also taken a look at who Jesus is and the importance of God's Word. You know what you stand for, but do you yet know *who you are?* God has clearly defined who we are in His Word, beginning in the first chapter of the first book. Genesis 1:27 says, "God created man in His own image, in the image of God He created him; male and female He created them."

From the start, we were created in the image of God. The Bible teaches us that He knew us even *before* we were made. Jeremiah 1:5 declares, "Before I formed you in the womb, I knew you." Your breath is His breath, and your life was created to mirror and glorify Him while intentionally being in a relationship with Him. Unfortunately, along the way, sin entered the picture and fractured our communion with God, and as a result, brought feelings of shame and worthlessness into humanity. In short, our sin is what throws us into an identity crisis. The only way out of that crisis is to saturate our minds and hearts with how God defines us.

What does it mean to be made in God's image? It means to "be holy as [He is] holy" (1 Peter 1:16). Being holy simply means to be set apart or to be different. The continuation of Jeremiah 1:5 from above says, "Before you were born, I sanctified you." Being set apart means that we show others the love of Jesus by loving our enemies, choosing joy, and disciplining ourselves to grow in the knowledge of God's Word. The bottom line is that we proudly bear the fruit of the Spirit in all parts of our lives. Living a Spirit-filled life sets us apart from a world filled with people in identity-crisis mode.

God calls us to be generous with our lives, and by opening up to others we will encourage others to open up to God (Matthew 5:13–16). Our purpose or mission in life is never about us. We were created to be light-bearers for Christ. Our call is to love and serve as Jesus loved and served. Today, I encourage you to allow the Lord to sanctify you and use your light to shine before others, bringing God's light into the world.

Reflection

1. When you look in the mirror, what do you see? Do you see someone who was made in the image of God, or do you speak to yourself in negative, less loving ways?

2. What does it mean to you to be made in God's image?

You Are Loved

For God so loved the world, that he gave his one and only Son, that whoever believes in him should not perish, but have eternal life.

—JOHN 3:16

God loves you, and His love for you is unconditional. In our humanity, we cannot imagine a love like this because we can never love perfectly. Just as we are incapable of loving with no bounds, no other human can love us on this level either. But God can, and He did when He sacrificed His only Beloved Son so that He could be in a relationship with you.

How deep is the Father's love for you? Ephesians 3:18–19 says, " … may be strengthened to comprehend with all the saints what is the width and length and height and depth, and to know Christ's love which surpasses knowledge, that you may be filled with all the fullness of God." God's love is so deep and wide for us that it takes a special kind of knowledge to even be able to begin to understand it. It is beyond our comprehension. However deeply your soul may have fallen into sin, depression, or rebellion, God's love is there and beyond. However far your offenses reach, God's love for you is there and even wider still. However high your unrighteousness reaches, His love is there and reaches higher. There's no place you can go to escape the loving arms of the One who created you.

How long will He love you? Jeremiah 31:3 says that God loves you with an everlasting love. We would call that "for eternity." Much like the amount of love He has for you, the length of God's love for you is immeasurable. And not only does God the Father love you, but His Son Jesus loves you so much that He voluntarily laid down His own life so that He could bridge the gap between you and God.

And God calls us to love others. Why? Because people in this world desperately need to know that they matter and are loved, just as I want to know that I matter and am loved. I pray that my family realizes every day that they are accepted for who they are, not for what they do or how many possessions they have acquired. Do the people around you believe they matter most to you?

I believe it is essential to share the love of God with those around you. Just as God's Word conveys His love for you and me, our words and actions convey the message of what matters most. So, let's make time to express the unconditional love of Christ to others.

Reflection

1. Can you think of a time when you felt unloved from being abandoned or making an unwise choice? Where was God? Have you done something that you believe God couldn't love you through? If so, name it here, and surrender it to Him.

2. Salvation is a gift to all who believe in the Lord, Jesus Christ. Reflect on John 3:16. What do these words mean to you?

You Are Adopted

But when the fullness of the time came, God sent out his Son, born to a woman, born under the law, that he might redeem those who were under the law, that we might receive the adoption as children.

—GALATIANS 4:4–5

God loved you so much that He sent His Son to die for your sins. Because Jesus willingly laid down His life for you, you have the privilege of being adopted into the eternal family of God. If you confess with your mouth that Jesus is Lord and believe in your heart that God raised Him from the dead, you are accepted into a never-ending family that transcends time, geographical boundaries and languages, and cultural differences. You, my beautiful friend, are God's child.

What does it mean to be adopted by God? It means that you gain access to all the rights and privileges associated with being part of a family. Your adoption is not based on your looks, your performance, or your status. You were saved by His beautiful grace. When you become a child of God, you are adopted by God, the perfect Father. He loves you, and nothing you do will ever change God's love for you (Romans 8:35–39). While sin can hurt your relationship with God, you can never lose your place as God's child.

As a child of God, you inherit both a new family for the remainder of your time on earth and a heavenly, eternal family. Here on earth, your new family is the Church. This is not to be confused with an earthly church, but the Church as Christ's Bride. Therefore, throughout your travels, as you meet other believers who have the Spirit of God living within them, remember that they are your brothers and sisters. How beautiful that God's family reaches to the farthest corners of the earth.

After this life, your heavenly family extends across all time to include believers who have gone before us from as far back as the creation of the earth.

Being adopted by God means being a co-heir with Jesus of an eternal inheritance. Romans 8:17 says, "And if children, then heirs: heirs of God and joint heirs with Christ, if indeed we suffer with him, that we may also be glorified with him." If Jesus is God's Son, and we are adopted children of God, then we are in line for the same inheritance of glory for all of eternity. The absolute opulence of our inheritance, an eternity spent with God in unimaginable heaven, is truly a gift from God!

Reflection

1. What has your experience with your earthly family been? How does it differ from being part of the family of God?

2. Reflect on your eternal inheritance, and journal your thoughts on the opulence of an eternity spent with God the Father.

You Are Accepted

*Therefore accept one another, even as Christ also accepted you,
to the glory of God.*

—ROMANS 15:7

We all crave acceptance. It's said that affirmation is widely known as an instinctual desire. Women especially seek connection, acceptance, and love, as one of our greatest fears is in not belonging or being accepted.

Unfortunately, many of us find ourselves unfulfilled in our quests for acceptance. We desire to be known, seen, and heard. We long for deep connections with other women for support and encouragement. However deep the desire may be, acceptance can be challenging for many, so we tend to seek approval in all the wrong places. For others, it may just be that they've given up looking for connection at all.

To be accepted is to be adequate or sufficient. When we are confident in who we are and whose we are, we are comfortable and free to be ourselves. As women of God, we must realize that genuine acceptance is God's acceptance. It has nothing to do with what others think or our inclusion in a group, but it has everything to do with having a strong relationship with God.

Placing our identity in God and finding our true acceptance is significant to who we are. Because God is holy and we are sinful, it was impossible for Him to accept us. His holiness simply could not coexist with our sin.

The good news is that Jesus made a way for us to be accepted freely! Romans 5:8 says, "But God commends his own love toward us, in that while we were yet sinners, Christ died for us." True acceptance means that the King of the world, holy and perfect, loves us unconditionally in Christ.

Once we understand that we are accepted, we can then accept other people from that place of security. This is powerful, my friends! If we were continually floundering, wondering who we were or whether anyone accepted us, we would never have the strength to love and accept others. But we have a foundation—a cornerstone in Christ—that anchors and propels us to share that same love with others. We are commanded to "therefore accept one another, even as Christ also accepted you, to the glory of God" (Romans 15:7).

Your life will be changed forever once you understand and embrace God's acceptance, as it truly is the only kind you will ever need!

Reflection

1. This week, take time to reflect on where you were before you came to know Christ. A reflection exercise I encourage my mentees to complete is journaling about where they were before Christ, where they are now, and how they got there. It's incredible to look back at our journey and discover just how far we have come in our spiritual growth.

2. Spend time in prayer sharing your gratitude with God, thanking Him for His love and acceptance. Be grateful for your journey, and know *you* are accepted, and *you* are not alone. God loves *you* unconditionally simply because *you* are in Him.

You Are Royalty

But you are a chosen race, a royal priesthood, a holy nation, a people for God's own possession, that you may proclaim the excellence of him who called you out of darkness into his marvelous light.

—1 PETER 2:9

Yesterday, we learned that God accepts us fully and that we are His children. Today, 1 Peter 2:9 tells us that we are a royal priesthood. God is King of everything, and we as His children are royalty. These words are so important to our identity and knowing whose we are. Why? Because God has made us in His image. From the beginning of time, He created us.

This verse describes who we are as individuals and as a group of believers, uniquely called to be Christ's servants. Thankfully, we are brought from our darkness into the light, and because of that, we are to share our testimony with others. Representing God is a theme throughout the Bible. When we are sure of our God-created identities, we glorify Him and become confident in the greater family, a holy nation, to which we belong. Because of this, we can live according to God's standards and not the world's, as we know who we are and whose we are.

Understanding this, how do you represent God to others? Do you glorify God through your words and actions? Do you posture yourself appropriately, or do you appear defeated? Do you stand tall on the foundation of God's Word, knowing that you are a reflection of the excellence of Him, who has called you out of darkness? You were not chosen for your own selfish desires, but you were anointed to be set apart in God's family of royal priesthood. How you use your time and talents can either direct people to or away from God. Ultimately, you were chosen and identified as His, and His Word is your assurance.

Beloved, I pray that you reflect on these words today and take to heart who God says you are because this is your unshakeable identity. You are chosen, you are a royal priesthood, you are God's own possession, and you are heir to an eternal kingdom with immeasurable resources. You, my friend, represent the Most High God and were saved for one purpose: to proclaim the good news of Jesus Christ.

Reflection

1. Your posture and attitude are a reflection of Christ. When others see you, do they see royalty, or do they see defeat?

2. In what areas of your life do you need to proclaim Jesus today?

You Are Free

For the law of the Spirit of life in Christ Jesus made me free from the law of sin and of death.

—ROMANS 8:2

The power of the Holy Spirit equips and empowers believers to live life in the victory of Christ. The Holy Spirit has set us free from the bondage of sin with Christ Jesus. But unfortunately, when we choose sinful behavior, we become entangled by our transgressions, which is precisely where Satan desires to see us.

Remember Eve? She was tempted, and in her weakness, the snake influenced her to question God. Fortunately, Eve took responsibility by admitting her sin to God, and due to her repentance, she experienced His grace. Because Christ set us free from sin and death, we too can experience God's grace and forgiveness when we disobey or make poor choices. We may still suffer the consequences of our actions, but we can experience forgiveness and restoration, just as Eve did, when we confess, admit, and believe.

The Bible says that He not only set you free from your sins, but He remembers them no more (Hebrews 8:12). You are justified in Christ, and to Jesus, you are clean of all thoughts, words, and actions offensive to God. John 8:36 declares, "If therefore the Son makes you free, you will be free indeed." That means the freedom from your sin is total and complete. There's not a shred of your sin that is allowed to cling to you in Jesus's eyes.

When you think about who you are, do you get hung up on what you've done? Does the guilt and shame of your past or present overwhelm you? Do you allow your mistakes to define you? Satan loves to use shame, especially on women, to keep us from fully realizing our identity in Christ. However, the Bible says, "There is therefore now *no* condemnation for those who are in Christ Jesus …" (Romans 8:1). These words are cause for rejoicing. Although we have sinned and fallen short of the glory of God (Romans 3:23), we are acquitted!

Does that mean that we can live however we want and be in good standing with God? Of course not. Sin enslaves us whether we're in Christ or not, and it is best avoided at all costs. So, while we make our best attempts at living sinless lives, we should instead practice walking in obedience to Christ as a grateful response to what He has done and continues to do for us.

Reflection

1. When you consider your past, and even your present, are you overwhelmed by shame and guilt? When these feelings invade your thoughts, remember what Romans 8:1 says: "There is therefore now no condemnation to those who are in Christ Jesus, who don't walk according to the flesh, but according to the Spirit." God has acquitted you from your sin, and you are set free. Use this time to surrender any shame or guilt to God, and confidently bask in the light of His unconditional love.

2. Maybe you've released part of your sin to God but still carry other parts. "No condemnation" is total and complete. Spend some time today confessing your sin to God. Ask Him to bring to mind any transgressions you are unaware of and give those to Him so that you may experience true freedom in Him.

You Are Powerful

You are of God, little children, and have overcome them;
because greater is he who is in you than he who is in the world.

—1 John 4:4

When you became a child of God, you were given the power of the Holy Spirit to dwell within you—the power of Jesus! *Holman's Study Bible for Women* further states that the believer's salvation has "staying power" as in 1 John 4:15, "Whoever confesses that Jesus is the Son of God, God remains in him, and he in God."

This power gifted to us when we received Christ as our Savior is used not for our glory or success but for kingdom building. The power that comes upon us should be used for God's glory. The Holy Spirit empowers us to boldly proclaim the Word of God. You are powerful through the gifts and blessing of the Holy Spirit for the purpose of witnessing to the world.

Matthew 28:18 says, "Jesus came to them and spoke to them, saying, 'All authority has been given to me in heaven and on earth.'" Jesus was stating that He has the authority to give eternal life to all whom God had given to Him.

Jesus holds the power. He is the Lamb of God in gentleness (John 1:29), and He is the Lion of Judah in might (Revelation 5:5).

Acts 1:8 reminds us that, as disciples of God, we need the power of the Holy Spirit, the spiritual power of the Spirit for kingdom building. "You will receive power when the Holy Spirit has come upon you. You will be witnesses to Me in Jerusalem, in all Judea and Samaria, and to the uttermost parts of the earth."

Jesus knew that for us to fully embrace who and whose we are, we would need strength to overcome. Our power comes from God's Word. Second Timothy 1:7 tells us God has not given us a spirit of fear, but of power, love, and self-control. Through the Holy Spirit, we can serve fearlessly because greater is He who is in you than He who is in the world.

My friend, as you fully walk in your identity in Christ, you will embrace the power of His Spirit within you, which is higher than anything that can ever overcome you. Amen.

Reflection

1. Reflecting on the words of 1 John 4:4, "Greater is he who is in you than he who is in the world," what do you now understand and recognize about the power you possess?

2. Is there a particular area in your life where God is calling you to step forward in bold faith to witness? Are you doubtful or struggling due to your fears or insecurities? Today, I encourage you to lift your requests to God in prayer and seek Him. Seek His strength and His power that resides in you. Meditate on God's Word, and allow His Word to speak to you and ensure you of the power and strength of the Holy Spirit that resides in you.

You Are Chosen

You didn't choose me. I chose you. I appointed you to go and produce lasting fruit, so that the Father will give you whatever you ask for, using my name.

—JOHN 15:16

$\mathcal{B}$e encouraged; God chose *you!* Just as Jesus shared these words with His disciples to encourage them, He also chose them to go out and bear fruit. And He has chosen us to do the same.

We learned from Galatians 5:22–24 that to walk in the Spirit is to produce good fruit. These qualities are love, joy, peace, patience, kindness, goodness, faithfulness, gentleness, and self-control, and as the redeemed, we are chosen to produce lasting fruit.

Jesus appointed each of us, and as God's children, we learned that we are called to be the salt and the light. Matthew 5:16 tells us that we are to be generous with our lives, as we encourage others to be generous with their lives. In doing so, He has equipped us to be His light to the world.

We are chosen to follow Jesus by laying our lives down for the sake of others. As His disciples, we are to disregard everything this world offers in pursuit of the eternal glory of heaven. This is what Jesus did, and He commands us to follow Him—wherever He goes.

Now, the reality is that we are still in this world, and until the day we are called home, we will live surrounded by daily brokenness and sin. Jesus reminded us of this when He prayed to the Father, "I pray not that you would take them from the world, but that you would keep them from the evil one. They are not of the world even as I am not of the world. Sanctify them in your truth. Your word is truth. As you sent me into the world, even so I have sent them into the world" (John 17:15–18).

As you reflect on John 15:16, what type of fruit are you producing? Keep in mind, we were not saved by good works but saved to do good works. God's love is in each of us as His believers. He has created us for a specific purpose—to love God and others. So take heart; we are equipped with God's strength to do just that—bear lasting fruit as we win souls to Christ.

Reflection

1. Describe in words how you feel, knowing God chose you to produce good fruit.

2. In John 15:16, Jesus tells the disciples that the Father will give them whatever they ask for in His name. Thank Him for choosing you and anointing you to bear good fruit for the purpose of winning souls to Christ.

You Are a Child of God

See how great a love the Father has given to us, that we should be called children of God! For this cause the world doesn't know us, because it didn't know him.

—1 John 3:1

People often ask me how I can be calm in moments of hardship. Whether I'm walking through a season of pain from rifts in close relationships or a child's health scare, my eyes continue to focus on my heavenly Father. In those times when I cannot see a way out of the darkness, my confidence remains anchored in Christ. His Word steadies me through life's trials and tribulations. Through the world's lens, my circumstances may seem dire, yet joy remains in my heart. My eyes are fixed on Jesus and not my hardships. The world may not understand this, but as a child of God, I know where my peace lies.

Faith is the most important factor in being a child of God. Faith is simple yet complicated. Through faith, we experience knowing the goodness of the Father in our hearts, even when our minds haven't entirely grasped the concept. Having faith allows us to see and understand God's provision in both past and present and, at the same time, trust we will have enough for the future.

Did you notice the contrast between childlike faith and grown-up faith? I don't think it is a coincidence that Jesus taught highly educated scholars and religious leaders about children and faith. I don't think it was a spur-of-the-moment decision when Jesus welcomed the little children to Him.

As I ponder what it means to be a child of God, I often think about God sitting in an oversized chair while I am sitting at His feet and resting on His every word. As I bring my sadness, joys, fears, and frustrations to the Father, He encourages my heart, covers me in shalom, and reassures me through His Word.

Although the world may not understand how I can sit peacefully when life seems to be crashing down around me, my brothers and sisters in Christ recognize the peace bestowed upon us as children of God. Just as my children are confident that my husband and I will provide for their needs, I am confident that my Heavenly Father will provide for every one of my needs.

Reflection

1. Children are often a reflection of their parents, in looks and in learned behavior. Since we are children of God, our heavenly Father is the perfect role model. "Therefore, be imitators of God, as dearly loved children … For you were once darkness, but now you are light in the Lord. Walk as children of light …" (Ephesians 5:1, 8–10). As a Christian, you represent the family of God. When you become a child of God, you'll begin to reflect God's image through your actions and words. How can you apply these words to your life moving forward?

2. What does it mean for us as children of God to know that "for this cause the world doesn't know us, because it didn't know him?"

You Are Appointed

Your eyes saw my body. In your book they were all written, the days that were ordained for me, when as yet there were none of them.

—Psalm 139:16

Our true identity is established before we are born. In Psalm 139:14 David writes, "I will give thanks to you, for I am fearfully and wonderfully made. Your works are wonderful. My soul knows that very well."

Our heavenly Father saw us before our bodies were fully formed in our mother's womb. No matter who we are on earth, where we went to college, who our friends are, or what our profession is, we are first and foremost God's creation. He's a perfect God who makes no mistakes. Therefore, we can rest assured that God established our identity in His mind far before we were ever conceived.

God declared that He made us in His image right from the beginning of time. The creation account of Genesis 1:27 states, "God created man in his own image. In God's image he created him; male and female he created them." God made humans in His image, and because His promises are true, we can rest assured and know that He has done the same for us.

So many of us run to worldly sources to determine who we are or what we should be. I will be the first to confess I am guilty on more than one occasion. We fall into the trap where we define ourselves by what we do, what we have accomplished, or what possessions we own. We may even base our identity on what people say about us, using their opinions and thoughts to describe who we are to others. It's frightening but true!

My sweet friend, your identity cannot be shaken. God established your biblical identity even before you were born; it is not contingent on your behavior or performance. Your role as a beloved child of God is not due to anything you did, so there is nothing you can do to lose it. It is rooted in God's unconditional love and acceptance, not your ability to perform or attain a certain standard.

We are imperfect women loved by a perfect God. We are called by God. Our identity is founded on Jesus Christ and His work—not our own doings. Amen.

Reflection

1. How do you embrace your identity in Christ? Are you accepting of who you are in Him?

2. Do you share with others what Christ has done in your life? Do you encourage women to embrace their identities in Christ, accepting who and whose they are?

You Are Saved

For by grace you have been saved through faith, and that not of yourselves; it is the gift of God, not of works, that no one would boast.

—Ephesians 2:8–9

God's grace and favor have saved us, and there is nothing we have done or can do to purchase our salvation. We may not boast of our good fortune because it is not our doing but from God's provision alone. We may not brag about our good works because He has saved us to do His good works. Through His love and grace, He has given us the beautiful gift of eternal life.

God's grace tells us we are loved, accepted, and worthy of His creation. So when you doubt who you are, remember that God loves you, you were created for His good purposes, and your identity is unshakeable.

Jesus loves you so much that He gave up everything to come to earth. He didn't come as a king, showered with riches and praise; He came as a baby, needy and helpless. He was born into a poverty-stricken family and was shamed by the public. He was undesirable in the eyes of people. Isaiah 53:2–3 states, "For he grew up before him as a tender plant, and as a root out of dry ground. He has no good looks or majesty. When we see him, there is no beauty that we should desire him. He was despised and rejected by men, a man of suffering and acquainted with disease. He was despised as one from whom men hide their face; and we didn't respect him."

As we reflect on these words, we recognize that being saved by faith is a beautiful gift from God. He accepts and loves us regardless of society's thoughts or standards. The love He has given us is priceless. Isn't it a delight to know that this gift of unconditional love and salvation is accessible to each of us through faith? Being saved by grace is an act of God. Because God is good, He saved us to bear good fruit and to love and minister to others.

God's perfect love is eternal. It is a love that will never let you go, that came to earth for you, died on a cross, and poured out its blood for you. He who is Love loves you more than you can ever comprehend, and He saved you.

God's saving grace is a bountiful gift of love and is the greatest gift of all.

Reflection

1. How do you define *grace*?

2. What does it mean for you to know you were saved by grace through faith and not of yourselves?

You Are Born Again

For you are all children of God through faith in Christ Jesus.
— GALATIANS 3:26

One of my favorite activities in spring is taking time to enjoy the blooming flowers and colorful monarch butterflies fluttering about in search of sweet nectar. As I take in the beautiful sights of the season, I am often reminded of what the metamorphosis process is like in our journeys as born-again Christians.

When we make the transformational decision to accept Christ as our Savior, we begin our journey of becoming Christ-followers.

Just like the caterpillar stage, where consumption is paramount, so is the beginning stage of being born again. The stirring of the Holy Spirit within our hearts allows us to draw close to Him and His Truth. We begin to feast on His holy, living scripture. We seek Him in the quiet places. We yearn to grow closer to Him as we learn more about Him, deepening our faith.

The chrysalis stage is essential. This is where the caterpillar begins to rest, digest, and transform into a beautiful butterfly. This is where we, as followers of Christ, begin to learn how to rest in the Father. As the cocoons of trials and hardship surround us, we reflect on the nourishment of His truth, His Word. It is when we rest in Him and not in our struggles that we become renewed, and our minds are refreshed.

And finally, the stage we all know so well occurs: the butterfly's emergence. In this stage, as we walk with the Father in our new identities as followers of Christ, we are called forth to break free from the ways of this world and share His beauty and transformational power with the world.

I don't believe we will ever outgrow any of these stages while we are on this side of heaven. However, the beauty within each of these three distinct stages empowers us to continually feed on His Word, to daily pick up our cross, and to share the gospel as we bring His presence to those in our influence.

Because we are born again, we have the freedom to break free from the cocoon of this world and flutter freely within His presence, experiencing life in the victory of Christ!

Reflection

1. It doesn't matter what you did or who you were in the past; Jesus forgives all your sins and transforms you into a new person. He gives you a new beginning to start writing a new story of your life (2 Corinthians 5:17). What can you do today to show your gratitude for your new life in Christ?

2. What does it mean to you to know that Jesus, in His lovingkindness, reached down and restored you to wholeness and holiness?

You Are Called

I pray not that you would take them from the world, but that you would keep them from the evil one. They are not of the world even as I am not of the world. Sanctify them in your truth. Your word is truth. As you sent me into the world, even so I have sent them into the world.

—JOHN 17:15-18

Have you ever felt like you don't fit in? Have you experienced moments of knowing there was something more for you out there? Have you ever come to the stark realization that this world is not your home?

I don't know if you've ever had these feelings, but I do know that if you are truly a believer in Christ, you will acquire a feeling of homesickness while living in this world. Why? Because we are called to live in the world but not to be of it.

Just before Jesus went to the cross, He told his disciples in John 12:25–26, "He who loves his life will lose it. He who hates his life in this world will keep it to eternal life. If anyone serves me, let him follow me. Where I am, there my servant will also be. If anyone serves me, the Father will honor him." Jesus made this very clear as He taught the disciples what it meant to not be of the world. Instead of following the worldly ways of striving and achieving to gain the approval of man, we are called as followers of Christ to give up our lives. We are called to follow Jesus and lay our lives down for the sake of others. We are called to disregard everything this world offers in pursuit of the eternal glory of heaven. That is what Jesus did, and He commands us to follow Him wherever He goes.

The reality is that we are still on this earth, and until the day we are called home, we will live every day in a broken world. But do not lose heart. Jesus spoke about this too. He prayed to the Father that He would not take them out of the world but keep them safe from evil. Being called doesn't mean you get to live in isolation from the world, but it does give you the strength to stand firm, never partaking in what the world offers you. And as you are sent into the world, it is essential to your faith walk to remember who and whose you are and anchor your identity in Christ.

Reflection

1. What does it look like when one conforms to the world? Is there a time in your life when you followed the things of this world and not the things of heaven? If so, write out these times in your life where you followed the things of this world and surrender these matters to God.

2. Where do you believe God is calling you to serve and minister to others? Take time to prayerfully listen to God as you seek His Word.

You Are Set Apart

For you are a holy people to Yahweh your God. Yahweh your God has chosen you to be a people for his own possession, above all peoples who are on the face of the earth. Yahweh didn't set his love on you nor choose you, because you were more in number than any people; for you were the fewest of all peoples.

—Deuteronomy 7:6–7

I can't help but think of Mary Magdalene, a woman who was devastated and tormented by many demons. Yet, with the touch of the Savior, she was delivered from all seven of the demons that possessed her.

While others saw a woman terrorized by spirits and labeled her as such, Jesus saw her true identity as a daughter of Christ. He saw her beauty, her dignity, and her strengths. So Jesus, in His lovingkindness, reached down and restored her to wholeness and holiness.

She was His *very special treasure*. Just like Mary, the Father sees us as His daughters. He sees the gifts bestowed on each of us by the Holy Spirit. Jesus sees our alabaster hearts and the aroma of the perfume of our sacrificial worship. He knows us intimately and yet, in our sinful nature, still sees the holiness placed within us when He went to the cross.

Our Father knows the thoughts that consume us and the struggles that confront us. He knows the addictions, negative feelings, and people-pleasing that we deal with daily as we attempt to cope with the challenges of the world. He understands the lies and taunts of empty promises that cloud our minds and the less-than-pleasant experiences we encounter daily. Yet He calls us His *very special treasure*.

My dear sister-in-Christ, may you know full well the love of the Savior, especially in your deepest valleys. May you understand that you have been set apart for the work ahead of you and that you have been planted in this generation for a kingdom purpose. You are holy and pleasing to Him.

Sweet friend, let me encourage you that even when we don't have it all together, Jesus sees us as His treasured beloved. So let's invite Jesus to touch the places we hide from society. Let's meet with Him in the dark places of our souls. And when it is too hard to communicate with words, let us fall to our knees and allow Him to come into our silence.

And then, may we arise as His holy and special treasure, good and pleasing to Him.

Reflection

1. I encourage you to spend time reflecting on the significance of the words in Deuteronomy 7:6–7. What does it mean to you to know that God has chosen you for His own possession?

2. As you spend time in reflection, is there an area of your life where God is calling you to be set apart? Are you walking in obedience to His call?

Time for Reflection

We were also assigned an inheritance in him, having been foreordained according to the purpose of him who does all things after the counsel of his will, to the end that we should be to the praise of his glory, we who had before hoped in Christ. In him you also, having heard the word of the truth, the Good News of your salvation—in whom, having also believed, you were sealed with the promised Holy Spirit, who is a pledge of our inheritance, to the redemption of God's own possession, to the praise of his glory.

—EPHESIANS 1:11–14

At the beginning of this series, we learned that most people identify themselves according to their occupation or status. Can you relate? Have you identified yourself by something you've accomplished or a material item you possess in order to be seen or recognized by others?

My sweet friend, know this, all this time, even from before you were born, you were known, seen, and heard by the God who holds the entire universe in the palm of His hand. This is the same God who sacrificed His own Son, on your behalf, to save you from your sinfulness, and that same Son willingly obeyed. That's how much

God wants to be in a relationship with you. This kind of love is the love with which He defines you.

As you continue to seek God, I encourage you to intentionally prepare by spending time reading, reflecting, and praying on God's Word every day. The more time you spend in the presence of God, the clearer God's Word will become to you. Find a safe space that is relaxing and pleasing that allows you to be at your best. Invite the Holy Spirit to speak to your heart and lead you as you seek His leading and guidance.

To further your spiritual growth, I've included ten reflection questions for additional study. These questions may also be used as journaling prompts. Remember, it is your journey. Be honest with yourself as you journal your thoughts. It is exciting to look back at our reflections and see just how far we've come in our spiritual walk.

Study Questions

1. How did you identify yourself in the past? Did you base your identity on your job title, status, education, or failures?

2. Who or what have you depended on to formulate your identity?

3. How does understanding your identity in Christ change the way you see yourself?

4. In what areas of your life are you already experiencing the freedom of your identity in Christ?

5. What areas of your past do you need to let go of to finally break free?

6. What daily habits do you need to develop to help you fully embrace your identity in Christ?

7. Are there parts of your life that you need to surrender to God? Are there strongholds that keep you from all God has planned for you?

8. On a continuum ranging from "I identify myself by the world's standards" to "I fully identify in Christ," where are you in your identity journey with Jesus?

9. In what ways can you share with others about your new identity in Christ?

10. Can you think of a recent time where the power of your identity in Christ helped you to navigate a challenging circumstance? How did you feel afterward?

As you go through the process of answering these questions, you may find yourself surprised by what you uncover. Most importantly, ask God to speak to you, and as you hear His voice, allow the words to flow, and take time to journal the meditations. Seeing your thoughts on paper can be very revealing. Receive God's Word and what He is speaking into you. Be confident, and trust in who you are and whose you are. Welcome your current season and lean into your calling.

I hope you embraced your biblical identity over the past thirty-one days. Believing that you were created in God's image establishes the foundation for you to stand firm in knowing who you are and whose you are. I pray you truly know how valuable you are to God. You are a daughter of the Most High God. You are loved, accepted, and chosen.

Printed in the United States
by Baker & Taylor Publisher Services